A CHILD'S GARDEN OF PRAYER

WRITTEN AND COMPILED BY

STEVE and BECKY MILLER

Paintings by Kathryn Andrews Fincher

HARVEST HOUSE PUBLISHERS
EUGENE, OREGON

A CHILD'S GARDEN OF PRAYER

Copyright © 1999 by Steve & Becky Miller
Published by Harvest House Publishers
Eugene, Oregon 97402

Library of Congress Cataloging-in-Publication Data
A child's garden of prayer / [compiled by] Steve and Becky Miller;
    paintings by Kathryn Andrews Fincher.
        p.   cm.
        Summary: A collection of over fifty prayers, classic verses, and
    Bible verses, including bedtime prayers, mealtime prayers, Christmas
    prayers, and prayers of thanksgiving.
        ISBN 0-7369-0117-5
        1. Children Prayer-books and devotions—English. [1. Prayers.]
    I. Miller, Steve, 1960- . II. Miller, Becky, 1960- .
    III. Fincher, Kathryn Andrews, ill.
BV265.C476   1999   99-12819
242'.82—dc21   CIP

Artwork designs are reproduced under license from © Arts Uniq´ ® Inc., Cookeville, TN and may not be reproduced without permission.
For information regarding art prints featured in this book, please contact:

    Arts Uniq´
    P.O. Box 3085
    Cookeville TN 38502
    800-223-5020

Design and production by Koechel Peterson & Associates, Minneapolis, Minnesota

Scripture quotations in this book are taken from the Holy Bible, New International Version ®, Copyright © 1973, 1978, 1984 by the
International Bible Society. Used by permission of Zondervan Publishing House. The "NIV" and "New International Version" trademarks
are registered in the United States Patent and Trademark Office by International Bible Society; The Living Bible, Copyright © 1971 owned
by assignment by Illinois Regional Bank N.A. (as trustee). Used by permission of Tyndale House Publishers, Inc., Wheaton, Illinois 60189.
All rights reserved; the New King James Version, Copyright © 1979, 1980, 1982 by Thomas Nelson, Inc., Publishers. Used by permission;
and The Contemporary English Version, Copyright © 1995 American Bible Society. All rights reserved. Used by permission.

Printed in United States of America.

99 00 01 02 03 04 /IP/ 10 9 8 7 6 5 4 3 2

It's never too soon to teach a child to pray. This is especially true if praying is to become as natural as breathing—and as simple and uncomplicated in a child's mind as is his own basic need for love. The sooner we can help a child see that the goodness in the world around them is a gift from God, and that God is worthy to be praised and thanked for it, the more the child will be secured on a path leading to peace and fulfillment.

Steve and Becky Miller's book accomplishes all that and more. It's full of short, simple, natural prayers that illustrate how conversations with our heavenly Father should happen. It provides the perfect tool to help a parent weave good habits of prayer into the fabric of the rapidly developing character of their offspring. It's the way I raised my own children and now that they are grown, they have not strayed from it. Read this book aloud and have fun training up your child in the way he or she should go.

Stormie Omartian

"Let the little children come to me, and do not hinder them;
for the kingdom of God belongs to such as these."

JESUS
THE BOOK OF MARK

Lord, Teach a Little Child to Pray

Lord, teach a little child to pray,

And then accept my prayer,

Thou hearest all the words I say

For Thou are everywhere.

A little sparrow cannot fall

Unnoticed, Lord, by Thee;

And though I am so young and small

Thou dost take care of me.

JANET TAYLOR

Bless My Home

God makes our home a house of joy,

Where love and peace are given;

It is the dearest place on earth,

The nearest place to Heaven.

JOHN MARTIN
PRAYERS FOR LITTLE MEN AND WOMEN, 1912

Before Prayer

We fold our hands and close our eyes,

And kneel down, when we pray,

So we can keep our minds and thoughts

Upon the words we say.

After Prayer

And then our eyes are open wide

To see what we can do;

Unfold our hands so we can help,

They can be useful too;

Rise to our feet, so they will run

On errands through the day:

We like to feel that we can help,

Each in our special way.

LOUISE MARSHALL HAYNES

A Morning Prayer

Early in the morning,

I look up to the sky.

I see the sunshine coming

And the birds all flying high.

Thank You, God, for a new day;

Thank You for giving me life.

I know You'll be my helper

All this day and through the night.

STEVE AND BECKY MILLER

"Your compassions...
are new every morning."

THE BOOK OF LAMENTATIONS

Make My Life a Little Light

God, make my life a little light,

Within the world to glow;

A little flame that burneth bright,

Wherever I may go.

God, make my life a little flower,

That giveth joy to all,

Content to bloom in native bower,

Although the place be small.

God, make my life a little song,

That comforteth the sad,

That helpeth others to be strong,

And makes the singer glad.

M. BETHAM-EDWARDS

A Happy Day Prayer

Thank You for each happy day,

For fun, for friends,

and work and play;

Thank You for Your loving care,

Here at home and everywhere.

The World, My Home

Thank You, dear God,

Oh, how I love to roam!

In this beautiful world

You've made my home.

A world filled with rivers,

valleys and trees;

A world alive with horses,

rabbits and bees;

A world painted with colors like blue,

yellow and green;

A world that changes from summer

to winter to spring.

Thank You, dear God,

Oh, how I love to roam!

In this beautiful world

You've made my home.

STEVE AND BECKY MILLER

*"The Lord God made the
earth and the heavens."*
THE BOOK OF GENESIS

Be Near Me, Lord Jesus

Be near me, Lord Jesus, I ask thee to stay

Close by me forever, and love me, I pray.

Bless all the dear children in thy tender care;

And fit us for heaven to live with thee there.

MARTIN LUTHER

A Prayer Before I Play

Now, before I run to play,

Let me not forget to pray

To God who kept me through the night

And waked me with the morning light.

Help me, Lord, to love Thee more

Than I ever loved before,

In my work and in my play,

Be Thou with me through the day.

Amen.

All Things Bright and Beautiful

All things bright and beautiful,

All creatures, great and small,

All things wise and wonderful,

The Lord God made them all.

He gave us eyes to see them,

And lips that we might tell

How great is God Almighty,

Who has made all things well.

CECIL FRANCIS ALEXANDER

Hear and Bless

Dear Father, hear and bless

Thy beasts and singing birds;

And guard with tenderness

Small things that have no words.

The Gift of Rain

Rain, rain,

Always there

When it's needed,

Through God's care.

Rain, rain,

Sign of love,

Gift of life

From God above.

The Gift of Sun

Sun, sun,

Always there

When it's needed

Through God's care.

Sun, sun,

Sign of love,

Gift of life

From God above.

We Thank Thee

For health and food,
For love and friends,
For everything
Thy goodness sends,
Father in heaven,
We thank Thee.

RALPH WALDO EMERSON

A Child's Psalm 23

The Lord is my shepherd;

He gives me everything I need.

He lets me rest in fields of green grass

and leads me to quiet places near the water.

He gives me comfort and strength.

He guides me in the right way,

as He has promised.

Even when life becomes scary,

I will not be afraid, Lord,

because You are with me.

You are my Shepherd, and I know that You will keep me safe.

ADAPTED FROM PSALM 23

Dear Father in Heaven

Dear Father in heaven,

Look down from above;

Bless Father and Mother

And all whom I love.

Jesus Loves Me

Jesus loves me! This I know,

For the Bible tells me so.

Little ones to Him belong;

They are weak but He is strong.

Yes, Jesus loves me!

Yes, Jesus loves me!

Yes, Jesus loves me!

The Bible tells me so.

ANNA B. WARNER

*"Love is very patient and kind...
Love does not demand its own way."*

THE BOOK OF 1 CORINTHIANS

A Prayer for Mom

Thank You, God, for my mother.

Thank You for
her soft touch,
her kind voice,
her gentle heart.

Thank You for
the times we spend together,
the hugs,
and her love.

Thank You, God, for my mother—
for giving her specially to me.

A Prayer for Dad

Thank You, God, for my father.

Thank You for
his strong care,
his kind wisdom,
his hard work.

Thank You for
the games we play together,
the fun,
and his love.

Thank You, God, for my father—
for giving him specially to me.

STEVE AND BECKY MILLER

A Prayer of Thanks

God, though You live in the sky,

I know You are not far away;

I know You look down with Your loving eye

When I kneel down to pray.

I thank You, God, with a grateful heart

For all Your wondrous ways;

I know from me You'll never part,

Thanks for blessing all my days.

A VICTORIAN PRAYER

An Eighteenth-Century Grace

Be present at our table, Lord;

Be here and everywhere adored.

Thy creatures bless, and grant that we

May feast in paradise with thee.

JOHN WESLEY

Which Are You?

In the woods close by our house
Live two little birds,
Each one sings its song to me,
But what different words!

One sings all day happily
In all kinds of weather,
One complains the whole day through—
Both right there together.

In the nearby bushes
One bird seems to say:
"Happy, happy, happy,
Happy all the day."

On a sunny tree-top
Sits the other one,
"Oh, dear me," it's sighing,
(Not a bit of fun.)

Happy heart or sad heart?
Whisper now to me
Which of these you'll copy;
I know which I'll be!

LOUISE MARSHALL HAYNES

Our Hands We Fold

Our hands we fold,

And heads we bow,

For food and drink

We ask Thee now.

Amen.

A Prayer at Night

Jesus, tender Shepherd, hear me;

Bless Your little lamb tonight;

Through the darkness please be near me;

Keep me safe till morning light.

All this day Your hand has led me,

And I thank You for Your care;

You have warmed and clothed and fed me;

Listen to my evening prayer.

"Sing to the Lord with thankful hearts."

THE BOOK OF COLOSSIANS

God Is Always with Me

When I wake up in the morning,

thank You, God, for being there.

When I go to school each day,

thank You, God, for being there.

When I am playing with my friends,

thank You, God, for being there.

And when I go to bed at night,

thank You, God, for being there.

Father, We Thank Thee

For flowers that bloom about our feet,

Father, we thank Thee,

For tender grass so fresh and sweet,

Father, we thank Thee.

For the song of bird and hum of bee,

For all things fair we hear or see,

Father in heaven, we thank Thee.

For this new morning with its light,

Father, we thank Thee,

For rest and shelter of the night,

Father, we thank Thee,

For health and food, for love and friends,

For everything Thy goodness sends,

Father in heaven, we thank Thee.

RALPH WALDO EMERSON

"*Call to me and I will answer.*"

THE BOOK OF JEREMIAH

Lamb of God, I Look to Thee

Lamb of God, I look to Thee;

Thou shalt my example be;

Thou are gentle, meek, and mild,

Thou wast once a little child.

Loving Jesus, gentle Lamb,

In Thy gracious hands I am,

Make me, Savior, what Thou art,

Live Thyself within my heart.

CHARLES WESLEY

Let Us Pray

Let us pray, for God loves us;

Let us pray, for God hears us;

Let us pray, for God is our God,

And we are all His children.

The Lord's Prayer

Our Father, who art in heaven,

Hallowed be Thy name.

Thy kingdom come,

Thy will be done,

On earth as it is in heaven.

Give us this day our daily bread,

And forgive us our debts,

As we forgive our debtors.

And lead us not into temptation,

But deliver us from evil.

For Thine is the kingdom,

And the power, and the glory,

Forever and ever!

Amen.

JESUS
THE BOOK OF MATTHEW

A Good Way

Let's see, dear God, I want to tell

You in a brand new way

"I love You!" but I cannot think

Of anything to say.

I know, dear God! I'll run and do

Something for someone, and

Then when You see me doing it

Of course You'll understand!

MARY DIXON THAYER

A Seashore Prayer

The tide comes in,

The tide goes out.

Time and time again

The waves all shout!

The sand is here,

The sand is gone;

But Your love so dear

Stays on and on.

STEVE AND BECKY MILLER

Two Little Eyes

Two little eyes to look to God,

Two little ears to hear His Word,

Two little feet to walk His ways,

Hands to serve Him all my days.

One little tongue to speak His truth,

One little heart for Him in youth.

Take them, O Jesus, let them be

Always willing, true to Thee.

A Prayer for
Family and Friends

Lord, behold our family here assembled.

We thank You for this place in which we dwell,

for the love that unites us,

for the peace accorded us this day,

for the hope with which we expect the morrow;

for the health, the work, the food, and the bright skies

that make our lives delightful;

for our friends in all parts of the earth. Amen.

ROBERT LOUIS STEVENSON

"Be joyful always."

THE BOOK OF 1 THESSALONIANS

My Joy, My Song

God of love,

God of grace,

You bless my life,

You bless my days.

From the earth

To the stars,

You are the King

Both near and far.

In my heart,

All day long,

You are my joy,

You are my song!

STEVE AND BECKY MILLER

Jesus, Friend of Little Children

Jesus, Friend of little children,

Be a Friend to me;

Take my hands and ever keep me

Close to Thee.

W. J. MATHAMS

We Are All Special

Father...

How fun it must be

For birds to fly;

To glide in the breeze

Up in the sky.

As I watch them soar,

I think of You—

Way up in heaven

Beyond the blue.

I sometimes have wished

That I could fly—

That I could have wings

To lift me high.

But then I wonder,

What of the birds?

Do they wish that they

Could speak with words?

When they look to me

From in the tree,

Do they wish to be

A child like me?

Thank You, dear Lord,

For helping me

To see we are all

So special to Thee.

STEVE AND BECKY MILLER

Easter Is Coming!

The sun is now rising,

The birds are now singing;

The flowers are blooming—

And Easter is coming!

Church bells are ringing,

The children are singing;

All shout, and shout again,

That Jesus is risen!

Oh, what a happy day;

All the earth's creatures say,

Our Savior is risen

And now lives in heaven!

STEVE AND BECKY MILLER

The angel said to the women, "Don't be afraid!
I know you are looking for Jesus.... He isn't here!
God has raised him to life."

THE BOOK OF MATTHEW

An Evening Prayer

Before I lay me down to sleep,

I thank You, gracious Lord,

For all Your kindness rich and deep,

And for Your loving words.

Oh! Keep me, Lord, and lead me right,

Nor ever let me stray.

I know You'll watch me through the night

And through the coming day.

Prayer for a New Day

Father, we thank Thee for the night

And for the pleasant morning light,

For rest and food and loving care,

And all that makes the day so fair.

Help us to do the things we should

To be to others kind and good,

In all we do, in all we say,

To grow more loving every day.

REBECCA J. WESTON

"The Lord watches over you."

THE BOOK OF PSALMS

What Is a Blessing?

A blessing's a gift from heaven above;
Filled with care, and all kinds of love.

A blessing, you see, is something that's nice;
What's more, it's free—it has no price.

A blessing can be a friend who is kind;
Someone who helps, and doesn't mind.

A blessing can be a person who shares;
Freely with others 'cause he cares.

A blessing can be the warmth of the sun,
A day in the park, just having fun.

A blessing can be the shade from a tree;
And a cool breeze from o'er the sea.

A blessing can be cookies and other
Given to me by my generous mother.

A blessing can be a cup of water
Given to me by my wonderful father.

Thank You, dear God, for these blessings and more,
I have so much to thank You for!

STEVE AND BECKY MILLER

God Is My Help

The earth, the sea, the air and clouds,

I know were made by Thee.

And though, dear God, You are so great,

I know You always hear me.

I put my trust in You, dear God,

I have no help but Thee;

Help my heart to keep Your laws,

Wherever I may be.

A VICTORIAN PRAYER

A Thank-You Prayer

I have the dearest little dog,

As clever as can be,

Before he has his bone to eat

He looks right up at me

And says "I thank you" ("bow-wow-wow!")

Before he eats at all,

And then he takes his bone away

Down by the garden wall.

I cannot let our "Frisky" dog

Be more polite than I—

Remembering "thank you" every time—

And so I really try.

LOUISE MARSHALL HAYNES

Praise Him!

Praise God from whom all blessings flow;

Praise Him, all creatures here below;

Praise Him above ye heavenly host:

Praise Father, Son, and Holy Ghost!

THOMAS KEN

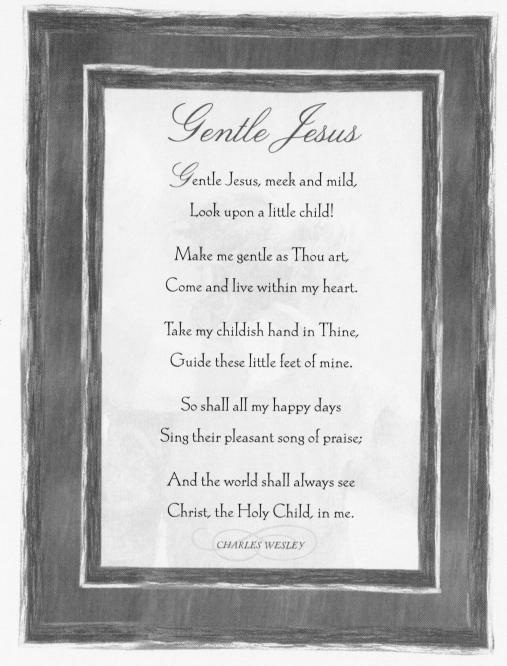

Gentle Jesus

Gentle Jesus, meek and mild,

Look upon a little child!

Make me gentle as Thou art,

Come and live within my heart.

Take my childish hand in Thine,

Guide these little feet of mine.

So shall all my happy days

Sing their pleasant song of praise;

And the world shall always see

Christ, the Holy Child, in me.

CHARLES WESLEY

Treasures and Pleasures

When Jesus was a child, I know
He shared His favorite toys—
I wish I were as generous
With little girls and boys.

There are some things I like to share
And even give away—
And other things I'd rather have
Myself when I'm at play.

But mother says it's selfishness
Unless I share them all;

I can spare many other things,
But I do love my ball.

And when we have a chance to go
To ride or anywhere—
A place I'd like to go myself—
My pleasures I should share,

And really try to be more glad
To have another go,
When there are seats for only three
And I make four, you know.

LOUISE MARSHALL HAYNES

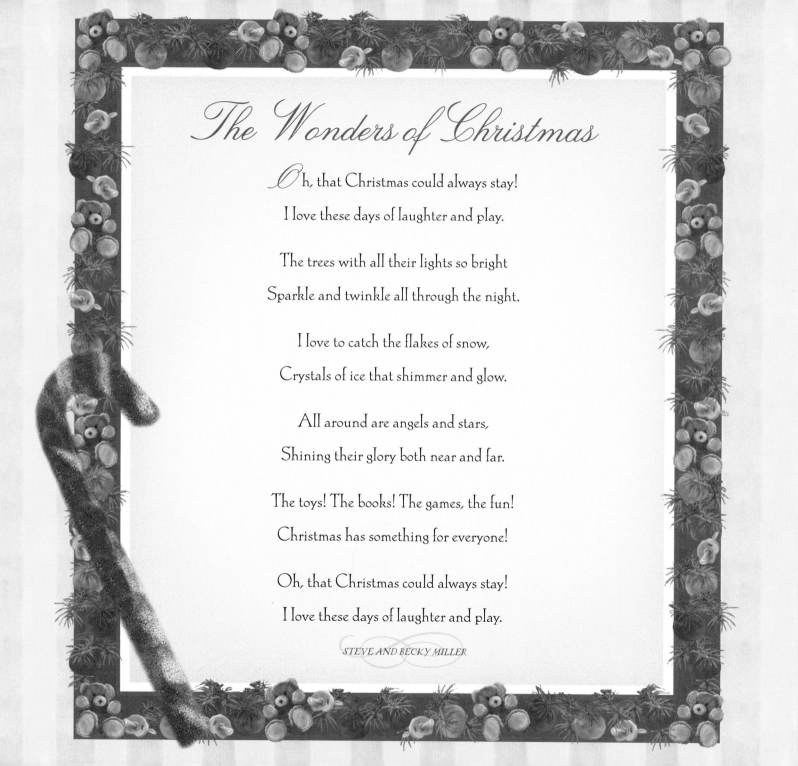

The Wonders of Christmas

Oh, that Christmas could always stay!

I love these days of laughter and play.

The trees with all their lights so bright

Sparkle and twinkle all through the night.

I love to catch the flakes of snow,

Crystals of ice that shimmer and glow.

All around are angels and stars,

Shining their glory both near and far.

The toys! The books! The games, the fun!

Christmas has something for everyone!

Oh, that Christmas could always stay!

I love these days of laughter and play.

STEVE AND BECKY MILLER

The Gift

What can I give Him,

Poor as I am?

If I were a shepherd,

I would bring Him a lamb;

If I were a wise man,

I would do my part.

But what can I give Him?

Give Him my heart.

CHRISTINA ROSSETTI

One L'il Child I Am

Five little toes You gave to me,

To wiggle at the end of each of my feet.

Four little fingers and a thumb

Did you know our hands, my friend, are so much fun?

Three l'il freckles You gave to me,

A special touch from You, Lord, for all to see.

Two l'il eyes for to see the world,

Oh, what a pretty gift to all boys and girls!

One l'il child I am, made by God,

And I know He loves me, a very whole lot!

STEVE AND BECKY MILLER

A Sleepytime Prayer

Lord, keep us safe this night

And quiet all our fears;

O bless and guard us while we sleep

Till morning light appears.

Now I Lay Me Down to Sleep

Now I lay me down to sleep,

I pray the Lord my soul to keep.

Guide me through the starry night

And wake me when the sun shines bright.

He's by My Side

I hear no voice,

I feel no touch,

I see no glory bright;

But yet I know that

God is near,

In darkness,

As in light.

He watches ever

By my side,

And hears my

Whispered prayer;

The Father for

His little child

Both night and day

Doth care.

"The Lord bless you and keep you."

THE BOOK OF NUMBERS

He Prayeth Well, Who Loveth Well

He prayeth well,

Who loveth well

Both man and bird and beast.

He prayeth best,

Who loveth best

All things both great and small;

For the dear God

Who loveth us,

He made and loveth all.

SAMUEL TAYLOR COLERIDGE

A Heartfelt Thanks

A very special thanks goes to both Bob Hawkins, Sr. and Ruth Samsel (both at Harvest House),

who were instrumental in developing the vision for this project . . . to Carolyn McCready, LaRae Weikert,

and Barbara Sherrill (also at Harvest House) for their wonderful support and encouragement . . . and

to Alta Herr, our church librarian, for her help in the research stage of this project.

PERMISSIONS AND ACKNOWLEDGMENTS

"Before Prayer" and "After Prayer," "Which Are You?," "A Thank-You Prayer," and "Treasures and Pleasures"—written by
Louis Marshall Haynes, excerpted from *Through the Church Door* (Boston: Wright and Potter Printing Co., 1924).

"A Good Way"—written by Mary Dixon Thayer, excerpted from *The Child on His Knees* (New York: The Macmillan Co., 1928).
Used with permission.

"Prayer for a New Day"—written by Rebecca J. Weston, excerpted from *Table Graces for the Family* (Nashville: Thomas Nelson, 1964).
Used with permission.

"Bless My Home"—written by John Martin, *Prayers for Little Men and Women* (New York: John Martin's Book House, 1912).